BALANCED!

(BE SMART ABOUT) SCREEN TIME!

STAY GROUNDED, SET BOUNDARIES, AND KEEP SAFE ONLINE

RACHEL BRIAN

LB

LITTLE, BROWN AND COMPANY
NEW YORK   BOSTON

FOR MILO.
MAGNVS ES! GRATIAS SUBSIDIO TVO.
TE MVLTVM AMO!

ABOUT THIS BOOK

The illustrations for this book were rendered digitally. This book was edited by Lisa Yoskowitz and designed by Carla Weise. The production was supervised by Bernadette Flinn, and the production editor was Annie McDonnell. The text was set in ConsentForKids, and the display type was hand-lettered.

Little, Brown and Company
Hachette Book Group
1290 Avenue of the Americas, New York, NY 10104
Visit us at LBYR.com

First Edition: November 2024

Little, Brown and Company is a division of Hachette Book Group, Inc.
The Little, Brown name and logo are registered trademarks of Hachette Book Group, Inc.
The publisher is not responsible for websites (or their content) that are not owned by the publisher.
Little, Brown and Company books may be purchased in bulk for business, educational, or promotional use. For information, please contact your local bookseller or the Hachette Book Group Special Markets Department at special.markets@hbgusa.com.

Library of Congress Cataloging-in-Publication Data
Names: Brian, Rachel, 1971– author, illustrator.
Title: Screen time! / Rachel Brian.
Description: First edition. I New York : Little, Brown and Company, [2024] I Series: Be smart about I Audience: Ages 6–10 I Summary: "An instructive comic guide to help children go online and use technology in safe and healthy ways." — Provided by publisher.
Identifiers: LCCN 2024000969 I ISBN 9780316575546 (hbk) I ISBN 9780316575706 (ebook)
Subjects: LCSH: Internet and children—Juvenile literature. I Internet—Safety measures—Juvenile literature. I Online etiquette—Juvenile literature. I Social media—Juvenile literature.
Classification: LCC HQ784.I58 B746 2024 I DDC 004.67/8083—dc23/eng/20240316
LC record available at https://lccn.loc.gov/2024000969

ISBNs: 978-0-316-57554-6 (hardcover), 978-0-316-57570-6 (ebook),
978-0-316-57571-3 (ebook), 978-0-306-83509-4 (ebook)

Printed in Dongguan, China

APS

10 9 8 7 6 5 4 3 2

WELCOME!

CONGRATULATIONS!

YOU'RE GETTING SOME SCREEN TIME. MAYBE EVEN A SCREEN OF YOUR OWN.

THAT'S SO

WOO!

MARBLE
YOUR AWESOME GUIDE

HI! I'M MARBLE.
I'LL BE POPPING UP THROUGHOUT THIS BOOK TO HELP YOU:

 HAVE FUN!

 PRACTICE CONSENT AND KINDNESS.

 STAY SAFE AND SET HEALTHY BOUNDARIES.

 KNOW WHEN TO GET HELP FROM AN ADULT.

3

CHAPTER 1 IT'S FINALLY HAPPENED!

YOU'VE DREAMED OF THIS GLORIOUS DAY . . .

AND IT'S FINALLY HERE—
YOUR OWN DEVICE!*

*OR ONE YOU GET TO USE.

A HUGE, EXCITING WORLD AT YOUR FINGERTIPS!

THERE ARE LOTS OF THINGS YOU CAN DO WITH THIS TECHNOLOGY, LIKE:

STAY IN TOUCH WITH FAMILY

PLAY GAMES

GET INSPIRED

FIND INFORMATION

BE ENTERTAINED

FIND NEW INTERESTS

BEING ONLINE MEANS BEING CONNECTED TO OTHER PEOPLE, IDEAS, AND EXPERIENCES.

POWER AND RESPONSIBILITY

A MINI COMIC ABOUT YOU AND YOUR DEVICE

YOUR SCREEN, YOUR RESPONSIBILITY.

CHAPTER 2 SEEING IS BELIEVING

OR IS IT?

OK, SO YOU'RE ONLINE. THAT MEANS YOU'RE CONNECTED TO LOTS AND LOTS OF **STUFF.**

YOU MIGHT HAVE ACCESS TO DIFFERENT THINGS DEPENDING ON YOUR DEVICE.

 CALLS

 GAMES

 TEXTS

 APPS

 WEB

SOME OF IT IS REALLY GREAT:

SMART IDEAS

HELPFUL INFORMATION

FUNNY VIDEOS

INSPIRING STORIES

ENTERTAINING GAMES

USEFUL TOOLS

WHAT to PICK?

DECIDING WHAT TO DO ONLINE IS A LITTLE LIKE DECIDING WHAT FOOD TO EAT.

YOU MIGHT PICK SOMETHING TASTY— LIKE AN APPLE. YAY!

BUT IF YOU EAT TOO MANY APPLES, YOUR BODY WILL FEEL CRUMMY.

AND IT'S THE SAME WITH SCREENS.

WATCHING ONE FUN VIDEO. YAY!

WATCHING VIDEOS FOR TOOOOO LONG.

Marble Says: **TAKE A BREAK!**

PAY ATTENTION TO HOW YOUR BODY FEELS. MAKE SURE TO GET OUTSIDE, MOVE AROUND, AND TAKE A BREAK!

CONTENT
TO STEER CLEAR OF ...

SCARY STUFF

EXAMPLES: VIOLENT VIDEOS OR THREATENING POSTS

SEXUAL STUFF

EXAMPLES: IMAGES OR VIDEOS WITH NAKED PEOPLE

NOTE ON NUDITY:
YOU MIGHT FEEL

CURIOUS, UNCOMFORTABLE, OR HAVE NO PARTICULAR FEELING ABOUT IT.

HMM...

YIKES!

WHATEVER.

THESE ARE ALL NATURAL REACTIONS. YOU CAN ASK YOUR PARENT OR A TRUSTED ADULT ABOUT WHAT YOU SAW AND WAYS YOU CAN EXPLORE THIS TOPIC SAFELY.

CONTENT

TO STEER CLEAR OF . . .

FALSE INFO
IT LOOKS
TRUSTWORTHY—
BUT IT'S WRONG.

SOMETIMES THE WRITER IS LYING:

OR THEY BELIEVE SOMETHING FALSE:

OR MAYBE IT'S A MIX:

DOUBLE-CHECK

WHAT YOU SEE ONLINE!

CONTENT
TO STEER CLEAR OF . . . .

TOO MUCH PERFECTION.

OUR PERFECT LIFE!

WOW, LOOK AT THAT KID'S ROOM!

WHAT AN AMAZING LIFE!

WHY DON'T I LOOK LIKE THAT?!*

* DID YOU KNOW THAT PHOTO FILTERS CHANGE HOW PEOPLE REALLY LOOK?

YOU AREN'T GETTING THE WHOLE STORY: EVERYONE'S LIFE HAS UPS AND DOWNS!

HURTFUL STUFF

YOU MIGHT SEE COMMENTS OR IDEAS THAT ARE RACIST, SEXIST, HOMOPHOBIC, OR JUST PLAIN MEAN.

YIKES!

TALK WITH A TRUSTED ADULT— YOU DON'T NEED TO DEAL WITH THIS ALONE.

HOW CAN PARENTS OR TRUSTED ADULTS HELP?

DISCUSS!

TALK REGULARLY ABOUT WHAT YOU'RE EXPERIENCING.

OPEN COMMUNICATION IS IMPORTANT.
IT ALLOWS YOU TO DISCUSS SHOCKING OR UPSETTING CONTENT
THAT YOU MIGHT HAVE SEEN AND TO GET SUPPORT.

SHARE THE EXPERIENCE.

WATCH SHOWS AND PLAY GAMES TOGETHER.

CO-WATCHING CONTENT IS A GREAT WAY
TO CHECK IN WITH YOUR FAMILY'S VALUES.

EXPLORE PRIVACY SETTINGS.

USE THE HIGHEST SECURITY SETTINGS— FOR EXAMPLE, SET UP MESSAGING ONLY WITH KNOWN CONTACTS.

MARBLE'S TIPS FOR GROWN-UPS

CHAPTER 3

LET'S GET SOCIAL!

HUMANS ARE SOCIAL. WE'RE WIRED TO CARE ABOUT BEING PART OF A GROUP. THAT'S HOW EARLY HUMANS SURVIVED!

IN GROUPS

GATHERED BERRIES

BBQ MEATS

MAKING STUFF

DOING GOOD!

ALONE

SABER-TOOTHED TIGER

UMMM

NOT GOOD.

WHEN WE'RE PART OF A GROUP, WE FEEL TERRIFIC!

WHEN WE'RE EXCLUDED, WE FEEL ROTTEN.

SOCIAL MEDIA GRABS OUR ATTENTION BECAUSE OF OUR IMPULSE TO CONNECT WITH OTHERS.

CARING ABOUT SOCIAL STUFF HELPS HUMANS FORM STRONG

COMMUNITIES

AND SOCIAL MEDIA ALLOWS US TO FORM CONNECTIONS WITH PEOPLE WE MIGHT NOT GET TO SEE IN REAL LIFE, LIKE:

FARAWAY FAMILY	PEOPLE WHO SHARE INTERESTS	PEOPLE SHARING NEWS OR TRENDS
NANA: WORKING ON MY GARDEN. COUSIN LILY: NEW PUPPY!	BEEKEEPER GROUP. MY NEW BIKE! SO COOL!	DID ANYONE SEE THE MOON TONIGHT? AMAZING! CHECK OUT THIS HAIRSTYLE!

BUT SOME PEOPLE HAVE TROUBLE TAKING BREAKS FROM SOCIAL MEDIA. THEY'RE AFRAID THEY'LL MISS OUT OR WON'T BE PART OF THE GROUP.

SOCIAL MEDIA
AND
YOUR BRAIN

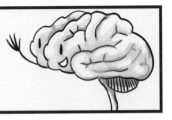

WHY IS SOCIAL MEDIA HARD TO QUIT?

YOUR BRAIN REACTS TO WHAT'S GOING ON.
WHEN A GOOD THING HAPPENS,
YOUR BRAIN RELEASES DOPAMINE.
DOPAMINE MAKES YOU FEEL <u>GOOD</u>!

AAHHH...

GOOD AND BAD FEELINGS WORK
A LITTLE LIKE A SEESAW:

FEEL BAD

LESS DOPAMINE

FINE

FEEL GOOD!

MORE DOPAMINE

WHEN THE SEESAW IS BALANCED—
YOU FEEL JUST OK.

WHEN YOU DO SOMETHING YOU ENJOY,
YOU PUSH DOWN ON THE "FEEL GOOD" SIDE:

HIGHER DOPAMINE AND FEELING GREAT!

15

YOUR BRAIN LIKES TO BE BALANCED, THOUGH ...
AND TO GET BACK IT PUSHES WAY DOWN ON THE
OTHER SIDE—NOW YOU FEEL KINDA BAD!

EVENTUALLY, YOU
COME BACK TO BALANCE:

BUT YOU HAVE TO WAIT A WHILE, AND IT'S
TEMPTING TO TRY TO GET THE GOOD FEELING BACK.

THE COOKIE JAR

A MINI COMIC

MMM ... FIRST BITE OF COOKIE— AMAZING!

YOU GET A BUNCH OF DOPAMINE AND IT FEELS GOOD.

ONCE THE COOKIE IS GONE, YOU MIGHT FEEL A LITTLE "MEH."

MAYBE ANOTHER COOKIE?

GOOD, BUT NOT AS GOOD AS THE FIRST COOKIE.

MAYBE ANOTHER?

BY THE FOURTH COOKIE, YOU JUST FEEL KINDA BAD.

THE SEESAW IS STUCK IN THE "FEEL BAD" POSITION FOR A WHILE.

TAKE A BREATH.

REMEMBER BAD FEELINGS DON'T LAST.

THE END

USING SOCIAL MEDIA CAN FEEL LIKE THAT

YOU WANT TO KNOW—DID PEOPLE CARE ABOUT WHAT YOU SAID? DID THEY LIKE IT? SOME DAYS YOU MIGHT GET A LOT OF POSITIVE FEEDBACK. OTHER DAYS YOU MIGHT NOT GET ANY.

THIS CAN TRAIN YOU TO CHECK
ALL THE TIME!

INSTEAD OF FEELING GOOD ALL THE TIME, IT CAN START TO FEEL BAD.
THE WAY TO FIX IT?

LIKING THE LIKES
A MINI COMIC ABOUT FEELING OK

THE END

Marble Says

TAKE A BREAK!

IF BEING ON SOCIAL MEDIA LEAVES YOU FEELING BADLY ABOUT YOURSELF,

IF YOU'RE ALWAYS COMPARING YOURSELF TO WHAT YOU SEE,

IF YOU FEEL SAD OR ANXIOUS ABOUT HOW PEOPLE RESPOND TO YOU (OR DON'T RESPOND),

AHHH!

TAKE A SOCIAL MEDIA BREAK!

DON'T WORRY, IT'S NOT GOING ANYWHERE.

HOW CAN **PARENTS** AND **TRUSTED ADULTS** HELP?

MARBLE'S TIPS FOR GROWN-UPS!

WAIT UNTIL AGE THIRTEEN TO GREEN-LIGHT SOCIAL MEDIA.

TALK ABOUT WHO TO FOLLOW AND HOW TO INTERACT KINDLY.

CHAPTER 4
STAY TRUE TO YOU!

WITH SO MANY PEOPLE,
SO MANY OPINIONS,
AND SO MANY OPTIONS ONLINE—

YOU MIGHT WONDER: HOW SHOULD **I** BE?

IF YOU'RE A KIND,
HELPFUL, AND HONEST
PERSON IN REAL LIFE . . .

TRY TO BRING THOSE
SAME QUALITIES TO
YOUR LIFE ONLINE.

DIGITAL (WITH) REAL
COMMUNICATION   PEOPLE

WHEN YOU SAY SOMETHING THROUGH TEXT, OR ANOTHER DIGITAL PLATFORM, IT MIGHT BE EASY TO FORGET THAT A REAL PERSON, WITH REAL FEELINGS, IS ON THE OTHER SIDE.

IF YOU SAY SOMETHING MEAN TO A FRIEND IN REAL LIFE

YOU'LL SEE RIGHT AWAY HOW HURTFUL IT WAS TO YOUR FRIEND.

IF YOU SAY SOMETHING MEAN ONLINE

YOU WON'T SEE THE OTHER PERSON'S REACTION.

AND YOU MIGHT NOT KNOW TO APOLOGIZE OR CHANGE YOUR BEHAVIOR.

TIPS TO STAY TRUE TO YOU

REMEMBER....

YOU HAVE **WORTH** AS A PERSON. WHETHER YOU HAVE 1 FRIEND ONLINE OR 1,000.

EVERY OTHER PERSON HAS WORTH TOO. YES, EVEN THE PEOPLE YOU DON'T LIKE.

TO LET GO OF OTHER PEOPLE'S OPINIONS OF YOU:
YOU DO YOU! ONLY TAKE FEEDBACK FROM PEOPLE YOU TRUST.

TO SET YOUR OWN VALUES:
DECIDE WHAT'S IMPORTANT TO YOU AND LET THAT GUIDE YOUR ACTIONS.

HOW TO FIGURE OUT YOUR
VALUES

 WHAT KIND OF PERSON DO YOU WANT TO BE?

 WHAT'S IMPORTANT TO YOU?

 HOW WOULD YOU WANT A FRIEND TO DESCRIBE YOU?

FUNNY · CONFIDENT · HONEST · KIND · LOVING · TRUSTWORTHY · SMART · FUN · CREATIVE · HARDWORKING · RESPONSIBLE · THOUGHTFUL · SILLY · BRAVE · CARING

ONCE YOU'VE IDENTIFIED YOUR VALUES,
THINK ABOUT HOW YOU CAN SHOW
THEM ONLINE.

OOPS!

WHAT TO DO WHEN YOU MESS UP

UH-OH!

EVERYONE MAKES MISTAKES.
IN REAL LIFE AND ONLINE.

USUALLY, A FEW SIMPLE STEPS CAN SAVE THE DAY:

APOLOGIZE—
AND REALLY MEAN IT.

I'M REALLY SORRY. I WON'T DO THAT AGAIN.

LISTEN—
TO WHAT THE OTHER PERSON HAS TO SAY.

LEARN FROM YOUR MISTAKE
( CHANGE YOUR BEHAVIOR!).

STAYING SAFE

IT'S IMPORTANT TO BE YOU ONLINE,
AND ALSO TO KEEP PRIVATE STUFF PRIVATE.

WHAT STAYS  ?

YOU CAN MAKE YOUR OWN LIST
WITH TRUSTED ADULTS, BUT HERE'S
A GOOD STARTING POINT.

DON'T SHARE:

 HOME ADDRESS
OR PHONE NUMBER

 YOUR SCHOOL INFO

 PASSWORDS

 DETAILS ABOUT YOUR
SCHEDULE

 IMPORTANT NUMBERS
LIKE CREDIT CARDS

REMEMBER THAT
WHATEVER YOU POST—
IT'S PERMANENT.

CHAPTER 5

ONLINE FRIENDSHIPS AND BOUNDARIES

THEY'RE GREAT!

HAVING FRIENDS ONLINE CAN BE A LOT OF FUN!

JUST LIKE IN REAL LIFE, IT'S IMPORTANT TO SET BOUNDARIES TO KEEP THESE FRIENDSHIPS

HEALTHY & SAFE.

WHAT'S A BOUNDARY AGAIN?

A BOUNDARY MEANS DECIDING

WHAT YOU'RE OK WITH. & WHAT YOU'RE NOT OK WITH.

BOUNDARY

EVERYONE HAS DIFFERENT BOUNDARIES.

IT'S ALL ABOUT HONORING YOURSELF
AND HOW YOU FEEL.

WHAT ARE MY BOUNDARIES?

 START BY THINKING ABOUT HOW THINGS MAKE YOU FEEL.

 EXAMPLES

FEELS *GOOD*

⭐ KIND WORDS

⭐ QUIET TIME TO MYSELF EACH DAY

⭐ CONNECTING WITH FRIENDS ONLINE

⭐ TRUST

FEELS **NOT** GOOD

❌ HURTFUL WORDS

❌ PRESSURE TO TEXT TOO OFTEN

❌ DEMANDING PASSWORDS

❌ USING GUILT

HOW TO SET A BOUNDARY IN
4 EASY STEPS

1 SAY WHAT YOU'RE **NOT OK WITH.**

WHEN YOU GOT MAD, YOU TEXTED "NOBODY LIKES YOU!"

I DID.

2 DESCRIBE HOW YOU **FEEL.**

AFTER YOU SAID THAT, I FELT SAD AND ANGRY.

OH...

3 EXPLAIN WHAT YOU **DO** WANT.

I WANT YOU TO TELL ME IF YOU'RE UPSET, BUT NOT IN A MEAN WAY.

OK.

4 DECIDE HOW TO **RESPOND** IF YOUR BOUNDARY IS CROSSED.

IF SHE KEEPS SAYING MEAN THINGS, I'LL CHOOSE NOT TO GAME WITH HER.

CAN YOU SPOT A BOUNDARY?

I SEE ONE!

A BOUNDARY ISN'T ABOUT CONTROLLING OTHERS—
IT'S ABOUT CHOOSING YOUR OWN ACTIONS.
SEE IF YOU CAN SPOT THE DIFFERENCE:

YOU SHOULDN'T HAVE ANY OTHER FRIENDS—JUST ME!

NO, THAT'S CONTROLLING!

I CHOOSE TO SPEND TIME WITH PEOPLE I TRUST AND WHO ARE NICE TO ME.

YES! GOOD ONE.

ALL MY FOLLOWERS SHOULD CUT THEIR HAIR! IMMEDIATELY!

YIKES! CONTROL ALERT!

NO RAINING ALLOWED.

NO . . . WWWW.

block

IF PEOPLE MAKE ME UNCOMFORTABLE ONLINE—I BLOCK THEM.

YES, GREAT IDEA.

HEY, MOM!

IF SOMEONE ASKS ME FOR PICTURES OR MONEY—I TELL AN ADULT.

YEP! YOU GOT IT.

YOU CAN'T CHANGE OTHER PEOPLE'S BEHAVIOR BUT YOU **CAN** CHANGE YOUR OWN RESPONSE...

HEY, HE CALLED ME NAMES!

WHAT CAN YOU DO TO STAY SAFE WHEN SOMEONE CROSSES A BOUNDARY?

ONLINE YOU CAN:

- ☐ ASK THEM TO STOP.
- ☐ REPORT THE PERSON TO A MODERATOR.
- ☐ BLOCK THEM.
- ☐ QUIT THE GAME OR CHAT.
- ☐ TELL A TRUSTED ADULT.

YOU STINK!

HEY!

ZIP!

NOW WHO AM I GOING TO BE MEAN TO?!

YOU CAN'T STOP SOMEONE FROM BEING UNKIND, BUT YOU CAN LEAVE THEM ALONE WITH THEIR UNKINDNESS.

A LOT OF US ARE TAUGHT TO "BE NICE!"

WE MIGHT NEED EXTRA PRACTICE LEARNING TO SAY "NO" AND TO SET HEALTHY BOUNDARIES.

"NICE" vs. KIND

- FEELS INSECURE
- AVOIDS SAYING NO
- DOESN'T SET BOUNDARIES
- WANTS TO PLEASE OTHERS
- SAYS WHAT THE OTHER PERSON WANTS TO HEAR

NICE

- FEELS CONFIDENT
- IS DIRECT
- IS CLEAR
- SETS BOUNDARIES
- USES KIND WORDS TO BE TRUTHFUL

KIND

SOME PEOPLE DON'T WANT TO ACCEPT "NO."

YOU HAVE TO, IT'S A CRISIS!

THEY MIGHT BE DRAMATIC,

IF YOU WERE REALLY MY FRIEND, YOU'D DO IT!

OR USE GUILT OR ANGER.

BUT YOU STILL GET TO SAY NO (AND MAYBE BLOCK THEM).

NEWS FLASH!

CONSENT ONLINE

CONSENT MEANS TO AGREE TO SOMETHING— ESPECIALLY IF IT HAS TO DO WITH OUR BODIES.

IN GENERAL, ASK PEOPLE FOR THEIR CONSENT BEFORE SHARING PICTURES OR VIDEOS.

SOMETIMES THERE ARE PICTURES OF NAKED PEOPLE ONLINE (AND ONLY SOME ARE CLASSICAL ART!).

BUT DID YOU KNOW IT'S ILLEGAL TO TAKE OR SEND NAKED PICTURES OF ANYONE UNDER THE AGE OF 18— EVEN YOURSELF?

SENDING ANY NAKED PICTURE MAY BE A FORM OF HARASSMENT.

UNLESS IT'S A CAT— WE'RE ALWAYS NAKED!

35

WHAT ABOUT OTHER PEOPLE'S BOUNDARIES?

SOMETIMES IT'S **YOUR** BEHAVIOR THAT'S CROSSING A LINE.

WHO ME?

WHA–?!

I WAS KIDDING!

SINCE PEOPLE'S BOUNDARIES ARE DIFFERENT, YOU MIGHT NOT KNOW YOU WENT TOO FAR.

IT TAKES COURAGE TO SET A BOUNDARY. **AND** IT TAKES COURAGE TO LISTEN TO SOMEONE'S BOUNDARY AND CHANGE YOUR BEHAVIOR.

THOSE JOKES MAKE ME UNCOMFORTABLE.

THANKS FOR SAYING SOMETHING. I'LL STOP TELLING THOSE KINDS OF JOKES AROUND YOU.

BOUNDARIES LOOK DIFFERENT DEPENDING ON AGE.*

LET'S SAY YOU WANT TO SHARE A FUNNY
MEME AND IT'S OK FOR KIDS YOUR AGE.

IT MIGHT NOT BE APPROPRIATE FOR A LITTLE KID.

AND IT'S NOT OK FOR OLDER TEENS OR ADULTS
TO SHARE ADULT-THEMED THINGS WITH YOU.

*KEEP IN MIND YOU MIGHT NOT KNOW THE TRUE AGE OF SOMEONE ONLINE.

ERNEST AND THE KITTIES

A MINI COMIC ABOUT HEALTHY FRIENDSHIPS

ERNEST WENT TO A FRIEND'S HOUSE FOR A VISIT.

ERNEST WANTED TO BE FRIENDS WITH <u>ALL</u> THE CATS. AFTER ALL, ERNEST WAS A KIND AND RELAXED DOG. BUT THE CATS HAD THEIR OWN IDEAS.

BIG KITTY WAS ANNOYED BY ERNEST.

SOMETIMES HE'D EVEN TAKE A SWIPE.

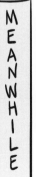

ERNEST NEVER EVEN SAW LITTLE KITTY. . .SHE GOT SCARED AND RAN TO THE BASEMENT.

BUT MINI KITTY L♡VED BEING AROUND ERNEST.

AND WHEN HE'D VISIT, THEY'D
SNUGGLE BY THE FIREPLACE.

AND ERNEST LEARNED:

YOU CAN'T BE FRIENDS WITH EVERYONE.
SPEND YOUR TIME AND ENERGY ON
THOSE WHO SHOW THEY ENJOY YOUR
COMPANY!

THE END

FRIENDS RESPECT EACH OTHER'S BOUNDARIES!

HEALTHY FRIENDSHIPS VS UNHEALTHY FRIENDSHIPS

⭐ YOU FEEL SAFE AND CONNECTED.

✖ YOU FEEL NERVOUS ABOUT HOW THEY ACT.

⭐ YOU BOTH HAVE OTHER FRIENDS AND ACTIVITIES.

✖ ONE PERSON IS JEALOUS AND CONTROLLING.

⭐ YOU RESPECT EACH OTHER'S BOUNDARIES.

✖ BOUNDARIES AREN'T RESPECTED.

CHAPTER 6

TROLLS, BOTS, AND **BULLIES**

THERE ARE MANY WONDERFUL AND KIND PEOPLE TO CONNECT WITH ONLINE.

THESE PEOPLE WILL:

SHARE OPINIONS RESPECTFULLY

USE KIND LANGUAGE

BE HONEST

THERE **MAY** BE A FEW PEOPLE
ONLINE WHO ARE JUST THERE TO BE UNKIND.

WE'LL BREAK THESE UP INTO THREE MAIN TYPES:

NOT LITERALLY, OF COURSE.
TROLLS ARE PEOPLE WHO TRY TO CREATE
CONFLICT AND GET PEOPLE ANGRY OR UPSET
BY POSTING CRUEL OR EXTREME COMMENTS.

THESE AREN'T ACTUALLY PEOPLE—
THEY'RE SMALL COMPUTER PROGRAMS
THAT POST THINGS—SOMETIMES BAD,
SOMETIMES JUST WEIRD!

WITH BULLIES, IT'S PERSONAL.
THEY WANT TO MAKE A PARTICULAR
PERSON FEEL BAD, AND THEY'RE USING
THE DIGITAL WORLD TO DO IT.

TOOLS TO COPE WITH BAD BEHAVIOR

TROLLS

THE GOAL OF A TROLL IS TO GET A STRONG NEGATIVE REACTION FROM TARGETS.

THAT'S SO MEAN!

HOW <u>COULD</u> THEY SAY THAT?!?

LIKE SADNESS   OR ANGER

THE BEST TOOL YOU HAVE IS TO

IGNORE

AW, WHY AREN'T THEY MAD?

THEY WILL USUALLY MOVE ON TO SOMEONE WHO REACTS.

IF THEY DON'T—TIME TO GO TO A TRUSTED ADULT FOR HELP.

DEALING WITH BOTS

IT CAN BE HARD TO RECOGNIZE A BOT BECAUSE THEY IMITATE HUMAN ACTIVITY— ESPECIALLY ON SOCIAL MEDIA.

BUT TRY NOT TO ENGAGE.

UMMM... DON'T ARGUE WITH A COMPUTER.

SAFETY TIP

DON'T CLICK LINKS!

ONLY GO TO TRUSTED SITES OR APPS.

ESPECIALLY IF YOU'VE "WON" SOMETHING OR IT'S A SCARY TEXT OR MESSAGE ABOUT AN ACCOUNT OR PASSWORD. TELL AN ADULT ABOUT THOSE KINDS OF MESSAGES.

DEALING WITH... CYBER BULLIES

CYBERBULLYING IS A FANCY WAY OF SAYING "SOMEONE WHO USES TECHNOLOGY TO BE MEAN TO SOMEONE ELSE."

1 RECOGNIZE BULLYING

— NAME CALLING
— SHAMING
— SHARING EMBARRASSING PICTURES OR VIDEOS OF YOU WITHOUT YOUR CONSENT
— MOCKING
— THREATENING

2 TAKE THE HIGH ROAD

IT MIGHT BE TEMPTING TO BE MEAN RIGHT BACK! BUT ... THEN YOU'D BE A BULLY TOO. REMEMBER YOUR VALUES AND WHO YOU WANT TO BE.

HIGH ROAD— FOLLOW <u>YOUR</u> VALUES.

LOW ROAD — ANGRY AND MEAN.

TAKE the HIGH ROAD

A MINI COMIC ABOUT CYBERBULLYING

GRETA WAS WALKING AROUND ONE DAY WHEN . . .

SHE TRIPPED ON A LOG!

EVA HAD RECORDED THE FALL . . .

AND SENT IT TO EVERYONE!

GRETA WAS ANGRY AND EMBARRASSED.

AT FIRST, SHE WONDERED HOW SHE COULD MAKE EVA EMBARRASSED TOO.

THEN SHE THOUGHT ABOUT WHAT KIND OF HEN SHE WANTED TO BE.

AND WENT TO PLAY WITH HER FRIENDS INSTEAD.

THEY DIDN'T CARE ABOUT THE VIDEO.

AND NEITHER DID GRETA. MAYBE IT WAS EVEN A LITTLE BIT FUNNY.

THE END

HOW TO BE AN ONLINE ALLY

SOMETIMES THE TARGET ISN'T YOU. IT MIGHT BE A FRIEND, A FAMILY MEMBER, OR A STRANGER.

NICE WORK!
YOU'RE GREAT!
GOOD JOB!
GO, YOU!

DROWNING OUT
NEGATIVE COMMENTS
WITH SUPPORT

CHECKING IN

STANDING UP
AGAINST THE BULLY

MARBLE SAYS:

IF YOU ARE, OR SOMEONE YOU KNOW IS, BEING BULLIED AND FEELING HOPELESS OR SO UPSET YOU OR THEY CAN'T COPE—IT'S TIME TO GET EXPERT HELP, LIKE A TRUSTED ADULT, RIGHT AWAY.

CHECK OUT NAMI.ORG FOR HELP.

47

MENTAL HEALTH SUPPORT

IF YOU'RE EXPERIENCING BULLYING OR YOU ARE WITNESSING UNKIND BEHAVIORS ONLINE—

IT'S IMPORTANT TO CONNECT WITH HELP IN REAL LIFE.

A COUNSELOR, THERAPIST, OR TRUSTED ADULT CAN HELP YOU SORT OUT YOUR FEELINGS AND YOUR OPTIONS. IT FEELS GOOD TO HAVE SOMEONE IN YOUR CORNER WHO SUPPORTS AND DOESN'T JUDGE YOU.

MORE OPTIONS

 SCHOOLS— TEACHERS AND ADMINISTRATORS

 ASKING SITES TO REMOVE CONTENT

 LAW ENFORCEMENT— TO REPORT ILLEGAL ACTIONS

 TRUSTED FRIENDS

TAKING CHARGE

CHAPTER 7

YOU'RE NOT THE BOSS OF ME!

TECHNOLOGY IS SUPERCOOL.
AND IT NEEDS TO FIT <u>WITH</u> YOUR LIFE IN THE REAL WORLD.

IT CAN OFFER YOU **NEW WAYS** TO DO THE THINGS YOU ENJOY

FUN ACTIVITIES AND EXERCISE

CONNECTING WITH FRIENDS

OR

TAKE TIME **AWAY** FROM THE THINGS YOU LOVE AND NEED.

ALWAYS INDOORS

NOT SPENDING TIME WITH FRIENDS

TOO LITTLE SLEEP

ANXIOUS WITHOUT SCREENS

YOU DON'T WANT TO GET **SWEPT UP** WITH YOUR NEW DEVICE AND FORGET TO SPEND TIME ON THE OTHER THINGS YOU CARE ABOUT.

FRIENDS

SCHOOL

HELLO?

GOALS

ACTIVITIES

FAMILY

BALANCING
YOUR LIFE IS THE KEY.

IDEAS

THINK ABOUT YOUR GOALS AND VALUES. HOW DO SCREENS FIT IN?

EACH FAMILY

HAS ITS OWN COMFORT ZONE AROUND SCREENS.

NO SCREENS   **LOADS OF SCREENS**

AND YOUR FAMILY MIGHT BE SOMEWHERE IN BETWEEN.

IF YOU'RE ABLE TO USE TECHNOLOGY TO
ENHANCE YOUR LIFE,
THAT'S GREAT!

KEEP AN EYE OUT FOR WAYS
IT MIGHT OVERTAKE
YOUR LIFE.

HOW MUCH TIME IS

THERE'S NO ONE ANSWER THAT'S RIGHT FOR EVERYONE, AND EACH FAMILY IS DIFFERENT.

HERE ARE SOME SUGGESTIONS: *

BABIES AND TODDLERS

UMM ... THEY DON'T NEED SCREENS AT ALL.

0 HOURS

3- TO 5-YEAR-OLDS

EDUCATIONAL AND FAMILY VIEWING

1 HOUR

6-YEAR-OLDS UP TO TWEENS AND TEENS

(NOT INCLUDING SCHOOL STUFF OR VIDEO CHATTING)

2 HOURS

* FROM THE AMERICAN ACADEMY OF PEDIATRIC

IT'S NOT JUST ABOUT **HOW LONG** BUT ALSO **WHY** YOU'RE ONLINE.

TIRED?

OOOH, PHONE...

BORED?

MMM...VIDEOS!

ANXIOUS?

CLEAN YOUR ROOM!

YA, IN A MINUTE!

bleep bloop!

SAD OR ANGRY?

ZONING OUT TO VIDEOS AFTER AN ARGUMENT

IF YOU USE TECH TO SOOTHE YOURSELF WHEN YOU FEEL BAD—YOU MAY FIND YOU AREN'T ABLE TO FEEL BETTER WITHOUT IT.

WHERE'S MY PHONE?!

53

ACTIVE vs. PASSIVE
SCREEN TIME

IT ALSO MATTERS HOW YOU INTERACT WITH TECHNOLOGY

ACTIVE USES THE DEVICE AS A TOOL.

PASSIVE LETS YOU ZONE OUT

LEARN A NEW SONG ON UKULELE

BINGE-WATCHING

LOOKING UP IDEAS FOR A RECIPE YOU WANT TO TRY

SCROLLING

ARE YOU THOUGHTFULLY CHOOSING ACTIVITIES—OR ARE YOU JUST FILLING TIME?

TAKE a BREAK

WITH MARBLE

IF YOU'RE FEELING ANXIOUS, IRRITABLE, OR SAD—OR IF YOU'RE HAVING:

TROUBLE SLEEPING

OOOH!

A HARD TIME FOCUSING

WAAH!

DIFFICULTY SOOTHING YOURSELF

GAMES, GAMES, GAMES . . .

UNWELCOME THOUGHTS

MARBLE SAYS:

MEH

UH-OH

OK

SCREEN-O-METER

THINGS ARE OUT OF WHACK! TAKE A BREAK!

I'M GREAT AT TAKING BREAKS—ME TIME.

SCIENCE CORNER

THE BENEFITS OF BOREDOM

BOREDOM IS, WELL, BORING. BUT IT'S GREAT TO GET BORED SOMETIMES.

WEIRD, RIGHT?

FEELING BORED CAN MOTIVATE YOU TO TRY NEW THINGS. AND IT HELPS YOU FEEL OK WHEN LIFE IS A BIT SLOWER.

YAY! READING TIME.

WAIT, WHAT AM I SUPPOSED TO BE DOING?

KIDS WHO SPEND A LOT OF TIME ONLINE, OR WHOSE ACTIVITIES ARE ALWAYS PLANNED BY ADULTS, NEVER GET THE CHANCE TO BUILD THE CREATIVE SKILL OF MAKING THEIR OWN FUN.

YOU HAVE TO PRACTICE!

SCREEN-FREE
BOREDOM-BUSTING
STRATEGIES TO GET YOUR CREATIVITY FLOWING

HERE ARE SOME IDEAS TO GET YOU STARTED.

MAKE A LIST OF STUFF YOU ENJOY
THAT DOESN'T REQUIRE A DEVICE OR AN ADULT:

BUG HUNT

DANCING

PAPER AIRPLANES

FORT BUILDING

READING

SNUGGLING PETS

ART

PRACTICING A SPORTS SKILL

GARDENING

STRATEGIES

TO KEEP SCREEN USE IN CHECK!

DINING ROOM TABLE

HOMEWORK TIME

NO SCREENS 60 MINUTES BEFORE BED

YOU DON'T NEED TO LOCK YOUR SCREENS IN A SAFE...

BUT YOU CAN HAVE SCREEN-FREE ZONES

AND SCREEN-FREE TIMES!

PARENTS AND TRUSTED ADULTS

MARBLE'S TIPS FOR GROWN-UPS!

CAN HELP BY:

PLANNING SCREEN-FREE ACTIVITIES

TALKING ABOUT MEDIA USE AND MAKING SURE THERE'S TIME FOR

SLEEP

PHYSICAL ACTIVITY

HEALTHY EATING

ENCOURAGING KIDS TO LEARN SELF-REGULATION
(HELPING KIDS FIND THEIR OWN BALANCE).

CHAPTER 8 — WHAT'S NEXT?

WHEW!

THAT'S A LOT OF INFO!

AND IT'LL TAKE TIME AND EXPERIENCE TO PUT IT INTO PRACTICE.

YOU DON'T HAVE TO HAVE IT ALL DOWN RIGHT NOW!

OH GOOD!

HERE IS A RECAP OF THE BIG IDEAS →

① ENJOY

POSITIVE EXPERIENCES
(AND TAKE CARE OF YOUR DEVICE).

EXPLORATION AND RESPONSIBILITY

ART
GAMES
INFO
FAMILY VIDEO CHATS
TEXTING WITH FRIENDS!

KEEPING IT CHARGED

KEEPING IT SOMEWHERE SAFE

BEING CAREFUL WHEN YOU HANDLE YOUR DEVICE

KEEP YOURSELF
② BALANCED

SOME DIGITAL STUFF

A LOT OF ACTIVE, SOCIAL, AND REAL-LIFE STUFF

REMEMBER: TECHNOLOGY IS JUST ONE PART OF LIFE!

FOLLOW YOUR
VALUES

3

DO YOUR BEST!

ACT ONLINE LIKE THE KIND
OF PERSON YOU WANT TO BE.

AND WHEN YOU MESS UP?

APOLOGIZE!
(SINCERELY)
AND LEARN FOR
THE FUTURE.

I'M REALLY
SORRY.

4 STAY SAFE

LOOK OUT FOR YOURSELF AND OTHERS.

KNOW WHEN TO
TAKE BREAKS

TECHNOLOGY CAN BE A FUN ADDITION TO YOUR LIFE. BUT LOOK OUT FOR SIGNS THAT YOU'RE OVERDOING IT:

ANXIOUS OR SAD

IRRITATED AND RESTLESS

THINKING ABOUT IT ALL THE TIME

LONELY OR SCARED

TAKE A BREAK AND MAKE YOUR OWN FUN:

GO FOR A WALK IN NATURE OR IN YOUR COMMUNITY.

HANG OUT WITH FRIENDS.

READ A BOOK.

TECHNOLOGY IS ALWAYS CHANGING:

DEVICES GAMES WAYS OF CONNECTING

BUT SOME THINGS STAY THE SAME:

CARING FRIENDSHIPS

HONESTY

KINDNESS

HEALTHY BOUNDARIES

SO, STAY TRUE TO YOURSELF AND SMART WITH YOUR SCREEN. YOU GOT THIS!

♥ 🐾 MARBLE!

☆ ACKNOWLEDGMENTS ☆

I'd like to warmly thank my three children for their unique perspectives and contributions throughout this process: to Milo for helping to pepper this book with insights gained from navigating online spaces, to Lola for providing cautionary tales and self-protective strategies, and to Enzo for calling me from college to encourage/harangue me.

To my editor, Lisa Yoskowitz, and to Alexandra Houdeshell, Gabrielle Chang, and the whole team at Little, Brown and Company: thank you for your brilliance, attention to detail, and patience. The final product is so much stronger for your efforts.

To my agent, Molly Ker Hawn at the Bent Agency—thanks for being great at everything I'm not.

RACHEL BRIAN

uses screens to make art and connect with people. She also enjoys taking breaks to walk in the woods or snuggle by a toasty fire. Rachel is the founder and CEO of Blue Seat Studios, an award-winning company that specializes in using humor to teach big ideas to kids and adults. Schools and organizations nationwide use Blue Seat Studios' animated content to foster conversations about consent, Title IX, anti-bullying, online safety, mental health support, and more. An entrepreneur and a former researcher, consultant, and educator, she's known for her work on *Tea Consent* and the book *Consent (For Kids!),* which has been translated and published worldwide. She is a graduate of Brown University and lives in Rhode Island.